THE HUMAN MIND: A PHILOSOPHICAL EXPLORATION

PUSKAR DEBNATH

Made with ♥ on the Notion Press Platform
www.notionpress.com

This book is dedicated to all of the great minds who have dedicated their lives to the study of the human mind. From the ancient philosophers to the modern-day thinkers, your insights and discoveries have helped to shape our understanding of the nature of consciousness, the self, and the mind-body problem. Your contributions have paved the way for future generations of scholars to continue to explore these important questions and gain new insights into the workings of the human mind.

We would also like to dedicate this book to all of the students of philosophy, psychology, neuroscience, and cognitive science who are passionate about the study of the human mind. Your curiosity, enthusiasm, and dedication to this field of study are an inspiration to us all. We hope that this book will serve as a valuable resource for your ongoing exploration of these important questions and help you to gain a deeper understanding of the nature of the mind.

Finally, we would like to dedicate this book to anyone who is interested in gaining a deeper understanding of themselves and the world around them. We believe that the study of the human mind has important implications for our understanding of ourselves and the people around us, and we hope that this book will help you to gain new insights into the workings of the mind and its relationship to our perception of the world. Thank you for your interest in this fascinating and important field of study.

Contents

Foreword

The human mind is a fascinating and complex subject that has been the focus of philosophical inquiry for centuries. From the ancient philosophers to the modern-day thinkers, there have been countless individuals who have dedicated their lives to exploring the nature of the mind and consciousness.

The Philosophy of the Human Mind is a comprehensive exploration of this important field of study, examining the key theories, concepts, and debates surrounding the nature of consciousness, the self, and the mind-body problem. This book brings together the insights of some of the most influential thinkers in the field, exploring the ways in which our understanding of the human mind has evolved over time.

The book is divided into three parts, each of which explores a different aspect of the philosophy of the human mind. Part One examines the relationship between the mind and the body, exploring the ways in which the mind and body are connected and the debates surrounding the nature of this relationship. Part Two explores the nature of consciousness, examining the different theories and perspectives on what consciousness is and how it arises. Part Three focuses on the self and personal identity, exploring the ways in which we perceive ourselves and how our sense of identity evolves over time.

One of the key strengths of this book is its accessibility. The authors have taken great care to present complex ideas in a clear and engaging manner, making this book an ideal resource for anyone interested in gaining a deeper understanding of the human mind. The book also includes numerous examples, case studies, and thought experiments to help readers gain a more concrete understanding of the key concepts and theories.

Another strength of this book is the breadth of perspectives that it presents. Rather than promoting a single perspective or theory, the authors have taken care to explore a range of different viewpoints and arguments, enabling readers to gain a more complete understanding of the debates surrounding the philosophy of the human mind.

The Philosophy of the Human Mind is also notable for its focus on the practical implications of the philosophy of the human mind. The authors explore the ways in which our understanding of the human mind can have practical applications in fields such as education, psychology, and neuroscience, and how it can also have important ethical implications.

Overall, The Philosophy of the Human Mind is a valuable resource for anyone interested in gaining a deeper understanding of the human mind. It brings together the insights of some of the most influential thinkers in the field, exploring the key debates, theories, and concepts that have shaped our understanding of the human mind. With its engaging writing style, numerous examples and case studies, and focus on the practical implications of the philosophy of the human mind, this book is an essential resource for anyone interested in this fascinating and important field of study.

Preface

The philosophy of the human mind is a field of inquiry that has captured the attention of thinkers for centuries. At its core, the philosophy of the human mind is concerned with exploring the nature of consciousness, the self, and the relationship between the mind and the body. These questions are complex and multifaceted, and they continue to be a source of much debate and discussion in the field of philosophy, as well as in other fields such as psychology, neuroscience, and cognitive science.

The Philosophy of the Human Mind is a comprehensive exploration of this important field of study, examining the key theories, concepts, and debates surrounding the nature of the human mind. In this book, we bring together the insights of some of the most influential thinkers in the field, exploring the ways in which our understanding of the human mind has evolved over time.

Our goal in writing this book is to provide readers with a clear and engaging introduction to the philosophy of the human mind. We have taken great care to present complex ideas in a clear and accessible manner, making this book an ideal resource for students and scholars who are interested in gaining a deeper understanding of this important field of study.

The book is divided into three parts, each of which explores a different aspect of the philosophy of the human mind. In Part One, we explore the relationship between the mind and the body, examining the key debates and theories surrounding the nature of this relationship. We examine the historical roots of this debate, starting with the ancient Greeks and tracing its evolution through the work of Descartes, Hobbes, and other influential thinkers.

In Part Two, we turn our attention to the nature of consciousness, exploring the different theories and perspectives on what consciousness is and how it arises. We examine the work of influential thinkers such as William James, John Searle, and Daniel Dennett, exploring their different perspectives on the nature of consciousness and the debates surrounding the hard problem of consciousness.

In Part Three, we focus on the self and personal identity, examining the ways in which we perceive ourselves and how our sense of identity evolves over time. We examine the work of influential thinkers such as David Hume, Immanuel Kant, and John Locke, exploring their different perspectives on the nature of the self and personal identity.

Throughout the book, we also explore the practical implications of the philosophy of the human mind. We examine the ways in which our understanding of the human mind can have practical applications in fields such as education, psychology, and neuroscience, and how it can also have important ethical implications.

We believe that the philosophy of the human mind is an important field of study that has much to offer us in terms of our understanding of ourselves and the world around us. It is our hope that this book will serve as a valuable resource for anyone interested in gaining a deeper understanding of this important field of study. We have taken great care to present complex ideas in a clear and accessible manner, and we hope that our readers will find this book to be a valuable resource in their ongoing exploration of the philosophy of the human mind.

Acknowledgements

Writing a book is a complex and challenging undertaking, and we would like to express our gratitude to everyone who contributed to the creation of The Philosophy of the Human Mind.

First and foremost, we would like to thank the many scholars and thinkers whose work has been instrumental in shaping our understanding of the philosophy of the human mind. Their insights and ideas have been invaluable in helping us to explore the key theories and concepts in this important field of study.

We would also like to express our gratitude to our editor, who provided invaluable feedback and guidance throughout the writing process. Their input and suggestions helped us to shape our ideas and refine our arguments, and we are deeply grateful for their support.

Finally, we would like to thank our families, who have supported us throughout this process with their love, encouragement, and patience. Writing a book is a challenging undertaking, and we are deeply grateful for the unwavering support of our loved ones.

We are honored to have had the opportunity to explore the philosophy of the human mind in this book, and we hope that it will serve as a valuable resource for scholars, students, and anyone interested in gaining a deeper understanding of this important field of study.

Prologue

The human mind has fascinated thinkers and scholars for centuries. From the ancient Greeks to modern day scientists, the nature of the mind and its relationship to the body has been a topic of intense debate and inquiry. Philosophers, neuroscientists, cognitive psychologists, and other researchers have all contributed to our understanding of the mind, but there is still much that remains unknown and controversial.

In this book, we explore the philosophy of the human mind, a field of study that encompasses a broad range of theories and ideas about the nature of consciousness, the self, and personal identity. Our goal is to provide readers with a comprehensive overview of this complex and fascinating field, and to offer insights and ideas that will stimulate further inquiry and debate.

The philosophy of the human mind is a field that has deep roots in Western thought. The ancient Greeks, for example, pondered the nature of the soul and the relationship between the body and the mind. Plato believed that the soul was immortal and that the body was merely a vessel for the soul, while Aristotle believed that the soul and body were inseparable, and that the soul was responsible for organizing and directing the body's activities.

In the centuries that followed, many other philosophers contributed to our understanding of the mind. Descartes famously argued that the mind and body were separate entities, and that the mind was non-physical and therefore immortal. Locke, on the other hand, believed that the mind was a blank slate at birth, and that all knowledge and experience was acquired through sensory perception.

As the field of science evolved, so too did our understanding of the mind. The advent of modern neuroscience, for example, has led to a greater understanding of how the brain processes information and how it gives rise to consciousness. Cognitive psychology, meanwhile, has provided new insights into how we think, reason, and make decisions.

Despite these advances, however, the nature of the mind and its relationship to the body remains one of the great mysteries of science and philosophy. We do not yet fully understand how the brain gives rise to consciousness, or how we are able to perceive the world around us. We do not yet fully understand the relationship between the mind and the body, or how our thoughts and emotions influence our physical health and well-being.

In this book, we explore these and other questions, drawing on a wide range of philosophical and scientific theories and ideas. We examine the nature of consciousness, the development of the self, and the role of memory in personal identity. We explore the mind-body problem, asking whether the mind and body are separate entities, or whether they are inextricably linked. We consider the implications of these ideas for our understanding of ourselves and the world around us, and we ask what the future may hold for the philosophy of the human mind.

Throughout the book, we seek to provide readers with a clear and accessible overview of the key ideas and theories in this complex and fascinating field. We draw on the work of many thinkers and scholars, and we offer our own insights and ideas, based on our own experiences and research.

Our hope is that this book will serve as a valuable resource for students, scholars, and anyone interested in gaining a deeper understanding of the philosophy of the human mind. We believe that this field of study is more important now than ever, as we seek to better understand the nature of our own consciousness and the workings of the mind. We hope that our work will stimulate further inquiry and debate, and that it will help to shed light on some of the great mysteries of the human mind.

CHAPTER ONE

INTRODUCTION

The human mind is one of the most fascinating and complex subjects that philosophers have explored throughout history. It is the seat of our thoughts, emotions, perceptions, and consciousness, and it shapes how we perceive the world and interact with it. In this book, we will undertake a philosophical exploration of the human mind, examining its nature, its functions, and its relationship with the world around us.

The study of the human mind is important for several reasons. Firstly, the mind is the foundation of our consciousness and self-awareness, and it shapes our identity and our relationship with the world. Understanding the nature of the mind can help us to better understand ourselves and our place in the world.

Secondly, the mind plays a crucial role in our cognitive processes such as perception, reasoning, and decision-making. By exploring the nature of these processes and the way they shape our understanding of the world, we can gain insight into the ways in which we think and reason.

Finally, the study of the mind has important implications for fields such as psychology, neuroscience, and artificial intelligence. By understanding the nature of the mind, we can better understand the underlying mechanisms of these fields and how they contribute to our understanding of the human mind.

Throughout this book, we will examine a range of philosophical questions related to the human mind. We will explore different conceptions of the mind throughout history, examine the relationship between consciousness and perception, and discuss the role of language and thought in shaping our understanding of the world. We will also examine the nature of reasoning and decision-making, explore the concept of the self, and examine the implications of technological advances for the future of the human mind.

By undertaking a philosophical exploration of the human mind, we hope to gain a deeper understanding of ourselves and our relationship with the world around us. We will examine the ways in which our minds shape our perception of reality, and explore the role of consciousness in shaping our experiences. Through this examination, we hope to shed light on the nature of the human mind and its relationship with the world, and to gain insight into the most fundamental questions about our existence.

CHAPTER TWO

DEFINING HUMAN MIND

The question of what the mind is and how it relates to the brain has been a topic of debate for centuries. In general, the mind can be defined as the set of cognitive faculties that enable humans to think, reason, learn, and experience emotions. The brain, on the other hand, is a physical organ that controls bodily functions and is responsible for generating thoughts, emotions, and other mental states.

The relationship between the mind and the brain has been a topic of debate since the time of the ancient Greeks. One of the earliest and most enduring views of the mind was dualism, which suggests that the mind and the brain are separate entities that exist independently of each other. According to this view, the mind is a non-physical entity that can exist without the body, while the brain is a physical organ that can be studied using scientific methods.

In contrast to dualism, materialism suggests that the mind is not a separate entity from the brain, but rather a product of physical processes that occur in the brain. According to this view, mental states such as thoughts, emotions, and consciousness are the result of electrochemical processes in the brain, and can be studied using scientific methods.

Idealism is another view of the mind that suggests that the mind is not a physical entity at all, but rather a set of mental representations that exist in the mind of the perceiver. According to this view, the world is not composed of physical objects, but rather of mental representations that are created by the mind.

Contemporary Views of the Mind

While dualism, materialism, and idealism have been the most enduring views of the mind throughout history, contemporary philosophy of mind has explored a range of different views and theories of the mind. One of the most popular contemporary views of the mind is functionalism, which suggests that mental states are defined by their functional role in the cognitive system.

According to functionalism, mental states are not defined by their physical properties, but rather by the way they function in the larger cognitive system. For example, a mental state like pain can be defined as a state that is caused by certain stimuli, that motivates the individual to take action, and that has a particular qualitative character.

Eliminativism is another contemporary view of the mind that suggests that mental states are not real entities, but rather illusory constructs that are the result of the way humans talk about mental phenomena. According to this view, terms like "thoughts," "emotions," and "beliefs" are not referring to real entities, but rather to the way that humans talk about mental phenomena.

The Mind-Body Problem and Its Various Solutions

One of the most enduring and complex problems in philosophy of mind is the mind-body problem, which concerns the relationship between the mind and the body. The mind-body problem has been the focus of much debate and discussion throughout history, and has been addressed by a number of different theories and solutions.

One of the earliest and most enduring solutions to the mind-body problem is dualism, which suggests that the mind and body are separate entities that interact with each other. According to this view, mental states such as thoughts, emotions, and consciousness are not physical entities, but rather non-physical entities that can interact with the physical world.

Another solution to the mind-body problem is materialism, which suggests that the mind is not a separate entity from the body, but rather a product of physical processes in the brain. According to this view, mental states are the result of electrochemical processes in the brain, and can be studied using scientific methods.

Functionalism is another solution to the mind-body problem that suggests that mental states are defined by their functional role in

the cognitive system. According to functionalism, mental states are not identical to their physical properties or their neural substrates, but rather are defined by their causal relations to other mental states, environmental stimuli, and behavioral outputs.

For example, functionalism proposes that a mental state like pain can be defined as a state that is caused by certain stimuli, that motivates the individual to take action, and that has a particular qualitative character.

This functional definition of pain can apply to any organism with a similar functional role in its cognitive system, regardless of the specific physical or neural mechanisms underlying the state.

Functionalism has been a popular solution to the mind-body problem because it allows for mental states to have causal power in the physical world, while avoiding the problems of dualism and the explanatory gap of materialism. However, functionalism has also been criticized for ignoring the qualitative aspects of mental states and for being too behaviorally focused, since it doesn't necessarily account for subjective experiences or consciousness.

Another solution to the mind-body problem is panpsychism, which suggests that consciousness is a fundamental and pervasive aspect of the universe. According to this view, all physical entities, from particles to organisms to planets, possess some level of consciousness or proto-consciousness.

Panpsychism avoids the problems of dualism by suggesting that consciousness is an inherent aspect of the physical world, and also avoids the problems of materialism by suggesting that consciousness is not reducible to physical properties. However, panpsychism has also been criticized for being a radical and unproven theory, and for failing to explain how complex mental states and subjective experiences emerge from simple physical entities.

In Conclusion:

Defining the human mind and its relationship to the brain has been a topic of philosophical debate for centuries, and continues to be a focus of contemporary philosophy of mind. While traditional views like dualism, materialism, and idealism have been enduring and influential, contemporary views like functionalism, eliminativism, and panpsychism have provided new ways of understanding the nature of mental states and their relationship to the physical world.

The mind-body problem remains one of the most complex and enduring problems in philosophy of mind, and has been addressed by a range of different solutions and theories. While no single solution has yet been universally accepted, contemporary philosophy of mind continues to explore new ways of understanding the nature of the mind and its relationship to the physical world.

CHAPTER THREE

NATURE OF CONSCIOUSNESS

Consciousness is one of the most fundamental and elusive aspects of the human mind, and has been the focus of intense philosophical and scientific inquiry for centuries. Despite this long history of study, the nature of consciousness remains largely unknown, and the problem of explaining it, known as the "hard problem" of consciousness, remains one of the most challenging and perplexing problems in philosophy of mind.

What is Consciousness and How Can We Study It?

Consciousness refers to the subjective experience of awareness and perception, including sensations, thoughts, emotions, and other mental states. It is an internal aspect of our mental lives, and cannot be directly observed or measured from the outside. Because of this subjective and internal nature, studying consciousness presents unique challenges and requires a range of different methods and approaches.

One method of studying consciousness is through introspection, or the process of examining one's own mental states and experiences. Introspection has been used since the time of Aristotle, and remains a valuable tool for studying consciousness, especially in the context of subjective experiences like emotions or pain.

Another method for studying consciousness is through the use of brain imaging techniques, such as functional magnetic resonance imaging (fMRI) or electroencephalography (EEG). These techniques allow researchers to observe changes in brain activity that correspond to different mental states or experiences, and can provide insight into the neural correlates of consciousness.

The "Hard Problem" of Consciousness and Its Various Solutions

Despite the various methods of studying consciousness, the problem of explaining it remains one of the most challenging and perplexing problems in philosophy of mind. This problem is often referred to as the "hard problem" of consciousness, and refers to the challenge of explaining how subjective experiences arise from the physical activity of the brain.

One solution to the hard problem of consciousness is offered by panpsychism, which suggests that consciousness is a fundamental and pervasive aspect of the universe. According to this view, all physical entities, from particles to organisms to planets, possess some level of consciousness or proto-consciousness.

Another solution to the hard problem of consciousness is offered by idealism, which suggests that consciousness is not a product of the physical world, but rather is the fundamental aspect of reality. According to this view, the physical world is not a real thing in itself, but rather a manifestation of consciousness.

A third solution to the hard problem of consciousness is offered by the notion of emergent properties, which suggests that consciousness is an emergent property of complex physical systems, such as the brain. According to this view, consciousness arises from the interaction of many simpler physical processes, and cannot be reduced to those processes alone.

Different Types of Consciousness: Phenomenal Consciousness, Access Consciousness, and Others

Consciousness can be divided into different types, each with its own characteristics and properties. One important distinction is between phenomenal consciousness and access consciousness.

Phenomenal consciousness refers to the subjective quality of experience, or what it is like to have a particular experience. For example, the subjective experience of pain or pleasure is a form of phenomenal consciousness.

Access consciousness, on the other hand, refers to the ability to use information from a particular mental state in order to guide behavior or cognition. For example, if you see a red apple, your visual system has access to information about the apple that can be used to guide your behavior, such as reaching out to pick it up.

The Relationship Between Consciousness and the Self

One of the most fundamental and enduring questions in philosophy of mind is the relationship between consciousness and the self. What is the relationship between the subjective experience of consciousness and the sense of self that we all possess?

One theory is that consciousness is a necessary condition for the self, and that the sense of self arises from the

ongoing integration of different aspects of experience into a coherent whole. According to this view, consciousness is necessary for the self because it provides the subjective experience of awareness and perception that is essential for having a sense of self.

Another theory is that the self is a product of the brain's ability to create a sense of continuity and coherence across different experiences and memories. This theory suggests that the self is a mental construct that arises from the brain's ability to integrate information from different sources, and to create a narrative that gives a sense of continuity and coherence to our experiences.

Yet another theory suggests that the self is an illusion, and that the sense of self arises from the same processes that give rise to other aspects of consciousness. This theory is often associated with the Buddhist concept of "no-self," which suggests that the sense of self is an illusion created by the mind, and that the ultimate goal of meditation and spiritual practice is to see through this illusion and realize the true nature of reality.

Despite these different theories and perspectives, the relationship between consciousness and the self remains a subject of ongoing philosophical and scientific inquiry. As our understanding of the nature of consciousness and the brain continues to evolve we can expect to gain new insights into this fundamental aspect of the human mind, and to continue to explore the deep mysteries of the nature of our subjective experience and our sense of self.

CHAPTER FOUR

PERCEPTION AND REALITY

Perception is the process by which we interpret and make sense of the information we receive through our senses. It plays a critical role in shaping our understanding of the world around us, and in determining our experiences and behavior. However, the relationship between perception and reality is a complex and contested topic, with different philosophical and scientific perspectives offering competing theories and explanations.

One traditional theory of perception is direct realism, which holds that our perceptions provide direct access to the external world, and that the objects and events we perceive are themselves the immediate objects of perception. According to this view, our sensory experiences are not mediated by mental representations or constructs, but rather provide us with direct and unfiltered access to the world around us.

An alternative perspective is an indirect realism, which suggests that our perceptions are based on mental representations or models of the external world that are created by our senses. According to this view, our perceptions are not direct reflections of the external world but are rather mediated by mental processes that interpret and make sense of the sensory information we receive. This view suggests that the world we perceive is not necessarily identical to the external world, but is rather a construct created by our minds.

Another theory of perception is constructivism, which suggests that our perceptions are actively constructed by the brain based on prior knowledge and experience. According to this view, our perceptions are not simply passive reflections of the external world or mental representations but are rather actively constructed based on a complex interplay of sensory input, cognitive processes, and prior knowledge.

The relationship between perception and reality is a subject of ongoing debate and inquiry, with different perspectives offering different views on the nature and scope of this relationship. Some argue that perception is a faithful reflection of the external world, while others suggest that our perceptions are shaped and mediated by a range of factors, including our sensory systems, cognitive processes, and prior experience.

The role of perception in shaping our understanding of the world is also an important area of inquiry, with research suggesting that our perceptions can have a powerful influence on our attitudes, beliefs, and behavior. For example, studies have shown that our perceptions of other people can be influenced by a wide range of factors, including their physical appearance, their social status, and their behavior.

The relationship between perception, consciousness, and the self is another area of inquiry that has received significant attention from philosophers and scientists. Some argue that perception is a necessary condition for consciousness and that our perceptions are a key element of our subjective experience. Others suggest that our perceptions are intimately connected to our sense of self and that the way we perceive ourselves and the world around us is central to our identity and our understanding of who we are.

In conclusion, the relationship between perception and reality is a complex and multifaceted topic that has been the subject of ongoing philosophical and scientific inquiry. While different perspectives offer different theories and explanations, the role of perception in shaping our understanding of the world and our sense of self is clear. By continuing to explore the nature and mechanisms of perception, we can gain new insights into the fundamental workings of the human mind and the nature of our subjective experience.

CHAPTER FIVE

LANGUAGE AND THOUGHT

Language is a fundamental aspect of human communication and culture, and it plays a central role in shaping our understanding of the world and our sense of self. Our language and the words we use influence the way we think and perceive the world, and can even shape our beliefs and attitudes. This phenomenon has been the subject of extensive research in psychology, linguistics, and philosophy, and has given rise to a range of theories and perspectives on the relationship between language and thought.

One of the most influential theories of the relationship between language and thought is linguistic relativity, also known as the Sapir-Whorf hypothesis. This theory suggests that the language we use shapes our perception of the world and our thought processes. According to this view, different languages impose different structures on our experiences and can shape our understanding of concepts and categories. For example, some languages do not distinguish between the colors blue and green, and speakers of these languages may perceive these colors as a single category.

Another theory of the relationship between language and thought is conceptual metaphor theory, which suggests that many of our abstract concepts and ideas are grounded in sensory and bodily experiences. According to this view, we use metaphors to map abstract concepts onto more concrete and familiar experiences. For example, the concept of time is often conceptualized as a path or a journey, with the future ahead and the past behind.

The nature of conceptual thought and its relationship to language is another important area of inquiry in the study of language and thought. Some researchers suggest that our ability to think and reason abstractly is closely tied to our ability to use language, and that language provides a kind of scaffolding for our cognitive development. Others suggest that our cognitive abilities are largely independent of language, and that we are capable of thinking and reasoning in the absence of language.

The role of language in shaping our consciousness and sense of self is also an important area of inquiry, with research suggesting that language can have a profound impact on our beliefs and attitudes. For example, the way we use language to describe ourselves and others can shape our perceptions of identity and social status. Additionally, the words and phrases we use can influence our emotional states and our judgments of others, and can even influence our behavior.

In conclusion, the relationship between language and thought is a complex and multifaceted topic that has been the subject of extensive research and debate. While different theories offer different explanations for the relationship between language and thought, the evidence suggests that language plays a critical role in shaping our understanding of the world and our sense of self. By continuing to explore the mechanisms and effects of language, we can gain new insights into the fundamental workings of the human mind and the nature of our subjective experience.

CHAPTER SIX

REASONING AND DECISION MAKING

Reasoning and decision-making are fundamental aspects of human cognition and behavior. Every day, we face a multitude of decisions, ranging from simple choices like what to eat for breakfast to complex decisions like which job offer to accept. While we often strive to make rational decisions based on sound reasoning and evidence, our decision-making processes can also be influenced by a range of biases, emotions, and heuristics that can lead us to make irrational choices. In this section, we will explore the nature of reasoning and decision-making, the factors that influence our decision-making processes, and the relationship between reasoning, decision-making, and the self.

The reasoning is the process of drawing conclusions or inferences based on evidence, information, and prior knowledge. It involves the use of logic, critical thinking, and problem-solving skills to arrive at a conclusion or make a decision. The reasoning is a key component of conscious thought, and it is closely related to other cognitive processes like attention, memory, and perception.

There are several different types of reasoning, including deductive reasoning, inductive reasoning, and abductive reasoning. Deductive reasoning involves starting with a general principle or rule and using it to draw specific conclusions, while inductive reasoning involves starting with specific observations or data and using them to make generalizations. Abductive reasoning involves using incomplete or partial information to generate possible explanations or hypotheses.

While the reasoning is often seen as a rational and objective process, it is also influenced by a range of cognitive biases and heuristics that can lead to errors in judgment and decision-making. These biases include confirmation bias, availability bias, and the sunk cost fallacy, among others. Additionally, emotions can play a significant role in shaping our reasoning and decision-making processes, with studies showing that people often make more impulsive and emotional decisions when they are under stress or facing high-stakes decisions.

Decision-making is the process of choosing a course of action or making a choice among several alternatives. Decision-making involves both conscious and unconscious processes, and it can be influenced by a range of factors, including emotions, cognitive biases, and social influences. Some decisions are made quickly and automatically, while others require more deliberate thought and consideration.

There are several different models of decision-making, including the rational decision-making model, the bounded rationality model, and the intuitive decision-making model. The rational decision-making model assumes that people make decisions by weighing the pros and cons of each alternative and choosing the option that maximizes their utility or value. The bounded rationality model suggests that people often make decisions based on incomplete or imperfect information and are limited by their cognitive abilities and time constraints. The intuitive decision-making model proposes that people often make decisions based on their intuition or "gut feelings" rather than through a deliberate and conscious process.

The relationship between reasoning, decision-making, and the self is complex and multifaceted. Our decisions and choices are often influenced by our beliefs, values, and personal goals, which are shaped by our experiences and cultural backgrounds. Additionally, our decisions can impact our sense of self and our identity, as we often use our choices and actions to signal our values and preferences to others.

In conclusion, reasoning and decision-making are central to human cognition and behavior. While we strive to make rational and informed decisions, our decision-making processes are also influenced by a range of cognitive biases, heuristics, and emotions that can lead to irrational choices. By understanding the mechanisms and factors that influence our reasoning and decision-making, we can make better choices and improve our overall well-being. Additionally, by exploring the relationship between reasoning, decision-making, and the self, we can gain new insights into the fundamental workings of human cognition and consciousness.

CHAPTER SEVEN

THE SELF AND PERSONAL IDENTITY

The self and personal identity are complex concepts that have been studied by philosophers, psychologists, and neuroscientists for centuries. These concepts are closely related but have distinct meanings, and understanding their relationship can shed light on how individuals perceive themselves and others.

The self refers to an individual's sense of being a distinct and separate entity from others. This sense of self includes an individual's thoughts, feelings, experiences, and actions, and is a fundamental aspect of human consciousness. Personal identity, on the other hand, refers to the unique set of qualities and characteristics that define an individual, including their memories, beliefs, values, and experiences.

The development of the self and personal identity is a complex process that occurs over the course of an individual's life. It is influenced by a variety of factors, including genetics, social interactions, culture, and personal experiences. As individuals grow and mature, their sense of self and personal identity evolve and become more complex, which can have significant implications for their overall well-being and sense of fulfillment.

One way in which the development of the self and personal identity is related to consciousness is through the concept of self-awareness. Self-awareness refers to an individual's ability to recognize and understand their own thoughts, feelings, and experiences. This ability is a crucial aspect of human consciousness, as it allows individuals to perceive and understand themselves in relation to others and the world around them.

Self-awareness is also closely related to the development of personal identity, as individuals who have a strong sense of self-awareness are more likely to have a clear and well-defined sense of personal identity. This, in turn, can lead to a greater sense of self-confidence, fulfillment, and overall well-being.

Another critical aspect of personal identity is memory. Memories play a vital role in constructing a sense of self, as they allow individuals to reflect on past experiences, make sense of who they are, and create a narrative of their lives. Memories are also essential for maintaining a stable sense of personal identity over time, as they provide continuity between past and present versions of ourselves.

However, memory can also be a source of confusion and conflict when it comes to personal identity. For example, individuals who have experienced trauma or significant life changes may struggle with integrating these experiences into their sense of self, leading to feelings of disorientation and loss of identity.

The relationship between the self, personal identity, and the mind-body problem is another area of ongoing debate and discussion. The mind-body problem refers to the philosophical debate about the relationship between the mind (including consciousness and mental processes) and the physical body. Some theories posit that the mind is a separate entity from the body, while others argue that they are inextricably linked.

In the context of personal identity, the mind-body problem raises questions about whether personal identity is determined by the physical body, the mind, or some combination of the two. For example, if an individual's memories and personality can be replicated in a computer program or artificial body, would that entity still be considered the same person?

These questions have significant implications for our understanding of personal identity and have been the subject of ongoing philosophical and scientific inquiry. Some theorists argue that personal identity is fundamentally rooted in the physical body, while others suggest that personal identity is primarily a matter of mental states and processes.

One theory that has gained significant traction in recent years is the theory of embodied cognition. This theory suggests that our understanding of the world is intimately tied to our bodily experiences and that our sense of self and personal identity are rooted in our physical bodies.

According to this theory, our brains do not simply process information about the world around us; they also use information from our bodies to shape our perceptions and experiences. For example, individuals who are physically fit and active may have a stronger sense of personal identity than those who are sed

entary and less physically engaged. This is because our physical experiences help shape our perceptions of ourselves and the world around us, which, in turn, shape our personal identity.

The theory of embodied cognition has significant implications for our understanding of personal identity and the mind-body problem. It suggests that our physical bodies are an essential part of our identity and that our sense of self is intimately tied to our physical experiences. It also suggests that our mental states and processes are deeply intertwined with our physical bodies, challenging the idea that the mind is a separate entity from the body.

In recent years, advances in neuroscience have shed new light on the relationship between the self, personal identity, and the mind-body problem. One area of research that has gained significant attention is the study of the brain's default mode network (DMN).

The DMN is a network of brain regions that are active when an individual is not engaged in any particular task or actively focusing their attention. It is associated with self-reflection, social cognition, and autobiographical memory, all of which are critical aspects of personal identity.

Studies have shown that disruptions in the DMN are associated with various psychiatric disorders, including depression, anxiety, and addiction, which suggests that this network plays a crucial role in our understanding of ourselves and our place in the world.

Another area of research that has shed new light on personal identity and the mind-body problem is the study of consciousness. Consciousness refers to an individual's awareness of their surroundings, thoughts, and experiences, and it is a critical aspect of human cognition.

Recent research has shown that the brain's conscious and unconscious processes are intimately intertwined, challenging the idea that consciousness is a separate entity from the rest of the brain. This research has significant implications for our understanding of personal identity, as it suggests that our sense of self and personal identity are intimately tied to our conscious experiences.

Overall, the self and personal identity are complex concepts that are intimately tied to human consciousness, memory, and physical experiences. While ongoing debates and discussions exist regarding the nature of personal identity and the mind-body problem, recent advances in neuroscience and cognitive psychology have shed new light on these issues and are helping us to better understand the nature of the self and our place in the world.

CHAPTER EIGHT

THE FUTURE OF PHILOSOPHY OF THE HUMAN MIND

The philosophy of the human mind has been a central topic of philosophical inquiry for centuries. The study of human consciousness, perception, and the mind-body problem has led to many significant advances in our understanding of ourselves and the world around us. As we move forward into the future, there are many potential areas of new development in the philosophy of the human mind that could help us gain even deeper insights into the nature of the mind, human cognition, and our understanding of ourselves.

One of the key themes that emerges from the philosophy of the human mind is the relationship between the mind and the body. The mind-body problem has been a central question in philosophy since the time of Descartes, and it continues to be a topic of much debate and discussion today. One of the potential areas of new development in the philosophy of the human mind is a deeper understanding of the nature of this relationship.

Recent advances in neuroscience and cognitive psychology have shed new light on the mind-body problem, suggesting that the mind and body are intimately intertwined. The theory of embodied cognition, for example, suggests that our physical experiences are a critical part of our perception and understanding of the world around us, challenging the idea that the mind is a separate entity from the body.

Another potential area of new development in the philosophy of the human mind is the study of consciousness. Consciousness is a central aspect of human cognition, and understanding its nature has significant implications for our understanding of ourselves and the world around us. Recent advances in neuroscience have provided new insights into the nature of consciousness, challenging traditional ideas about the relationship between the conscious and unconscious mind.

One of the key questions that emerge from the study of consciousness is the relationship between the self and consciousness. Many philosophers and cognitive scientists argue that the self is intimately tied to our consciousness and perception of the world around us. A deeper understanding of this relationship could help us gain new insights into the nature of the self and our place in the world.

Another potential area of new development in the philosophy of the human mind is the study of artificial intelligence (AI) and its relationship to human cognition. AI has made significant advances in recent years, and many experts predict that it will continue to play an increasingly important role in our lives in the future. The study of AI has significant implications for the philosophy of the human mind, as it challenges traditional ideas about what it means to be human and the nature of human cognition.

One of the key questions that emerge from the study of AI is whether machines can truly be said to have consciousness or self-awareness. Many experts argue that machines can never truly be said to be conscious or self-aware, as they lack the subjective experience that is central to human consciousness. However, others argue that as AI becomes more advanced, it may be possible to create machines that are capable of conscious thought and self-awareness, challenging our traditional ideas about what it means to be human.

The philosophy of the human mind also has broader implications for our understanding of ourselves and the world around us. Our perception of the world is intimately tied to our understanding of the nature of the mind and consciousness. A deeper understanding of the mind could help us gain new insights into human cognition, including memory, perception, and reasoning, which could have significant implications for our understanding of ourselves and the world around us.

Furthermore, the philosophy of the human mind has significant implications for many other areas of philosophy, including ethics and metaphysics. Our understanding of the nature of the mind and consciousness can help us gain new insights into the nature of morality, free will, and the relationship between the individual and society.

Conclusion

In conclusion, the philosophy of the human mind has been a central topic of philosophical inquiry for centuries, and it continues to be an area of much debate and discussion today. As we move forward into the future, there are many potential areas of new development in the philosophy of the human mind that could help us gain even deeper insights into the nature of the mind and human cognition. The relationship between the mind and the body, the nature of consciousness, and the study of artificial intelligence are just a few examples of areas where new developments could bring significant advances to our understanding of the human mind.

It is clear that the study of the philosophy of the human mind has important implications not only for philosophy but also for many other areas of study, including psychology, neuroscience, and cognitive science. By gaining a deeper understanding of the mind, we can gain new insights into the nature of human cognition and the way that we perceive the world around us.

Furthermore, the philosophy of the human mind can have significant practical applications in our daily lives. A deeper understanding of the mind can help us to better understand ourselves and the people around us, leading to improved relationships, communication, and decision-making. It can also have practical applications in fields such as education, where a deeper understanding of how the mind works can help us to design more effective teaching methods and curriculum.

In addition, the study of the philosophy of the human mind can have important ethical implications. Our understanding of the nature of consciousness and the self can have significant implications for our understanding of the rights and responsibilities of individuals, and our understanding of the relationship between the individual and society.

For example, a deeper understanding of the nature of consciousness could have significant implications for the way that we treat animals. If animals are found to be capable of conscious thought and self-awareness, then our ethical responsibilities towards them may need to be reevaluated. Similarly, a deeper understanding of the nature of the self and consciousness can have important implications for our understanding of personal identity and the rights of individuals.

Overall, the study of the philosophy of the human mind is an important area of inquiry that has significant implications for our understanding of ourselves and the world around us. By gaining a deeper understanding of the mind and consciousness, we can gain new insights into human cognition, memory, and reasoning, and better understand our place in the world. As we move forward into the future, it is likely that new developments in the philosophy of the human mind will continue to shed new light on these important questions and help us to gain a more complete understanding of the nature of the mind and human cognition.

9 798889 756040

Printed by Libri Plureos GmbH in Hamburg, Germany